We All Have

Sacred Spaces

Rev. Vicki Michela Garlock, Ph.D.

ISBN: 978-1-947486-16-4

Dedication

To my parents
Jan and Fred Michela
who introduced me to all sorts of sacred spaces

Table of Contents

Introduction

Have you ever looked at all the beautiful people in the world? It's amazing how different we are!

Hair is the perfect example. You can have blond curly hair. Or straight black hair. You can have long red hair. Or short brown hair.

You can hold it with ribbons, barrettes or headbands.

You can wear it in a ponytail or braids.

You can even dye it.

Have you ever seen someone with hair that was purple? Or green? Or blue?

Your hair can even be a crazy combination of things. And if you're bald, your hair can be nothing at all!

But it's not just hair that makes us one-of-a-kind.

The languages we speak are different.

Our eyes and skin come in various colors and shades.

Some of us walk on two legs while others use a cane or wheelchair.

And we wear different styles of clothing.

People are also different on the inside.

Some people are quiet and shy. Others talk a lot and act silly.

Some people like to be outside, while some prefer to be inside.

We listen to different kinds of music and eat different foods.

People even have different ideas about the meaning of life. These ways of thinking are sometimes called religions or faith traditions.

Most faith traditions have stories and rituals that have been handed down from generation to generation.

Usually, faith traditions also have spiritual leaders who serve as teachers and guides. They remind their followers to live a life of kindness and to show compassion to the earth and all its creatures.

Some religions also talk about forces beyond what we can see and hear. Those forces might be called gods and goddesses, good and evil, cosmic law, or just God.

But even if the beliefs are different, nearly all faith traditions have special places where believers can come together to pray, light candles, sing, meditate, dance, make offerings to **deities,** or participate in ceremonies.

Like people, these sacred spaces are all different.

Some are big.

Some are small.

Some are very old.

Some are brand new.

Some are fancy.

Some are plain.

Some have lots of things inside. And some are mostly empty space!

But each sacred space, no matter what it looks like, is special to the people who worship there.

Indigenous Sites

The very first sacred spaces were outside. Since people were closely connected to their environments, they met outdoors – in nature – for ceremonies and rituals.

*Mount Mayon is an active volcano in the Philippines. Many **Indigenous** people of the region consider it home to their supreme **deity,** Gugurang.*

Mountains and volcanoes – which are very large and can be seen from far away – are often considered holy. People tell stories about how the mountain or volcano came to be. Sometimes, if they view the peak as the home of a **deity,** they bring food and flowers as offerings.

According to legend, this Wave Rock in Australia was created during Dreamtime when Rainbow Serpent dragged her bloated body over the land after drinking all the water.

Unique landscapes also serve as sacred spaces. Mystical forests, winding rivers, half-hidden caves, special trees, unusual rock formations, and mysterious hot water springs all offered places where people could gather together to honor the earth or gods and goddesses.

Sometimes, people added their own special touches to these spaces. Cave walls could be painted with natural dyes, stones could be arranged in precise ways, and interesting sites could be marked with special paths.

This ancient cave painting is found in Mexico. Carbon dating indicates that some paintings in this region are 7,500 years old.

Eventually, people created even more well-defined gathering spaces by building walls or other shelters out of rocks, mud, or wood.

Ceremonies and rituals performed in the outdoors are as diverse as the places themselves. Sometimes, people sing, dance, or play drums. Sometimes, everyone gathers around a fire to share ancient stories about the ancestor world or lessons learned from the animal kingdom.

Sometimes natural elements, like fire or water, are used for rituals. And sometimes, tribal wisdom-keepers, often called **elders,** wear masks to bring the spirit world and the human world closer together.

These spiritual practices are often called **Indigenous** traditions. The word **"indigenous"** refers to people who lived on the land first, before settlers arrived from other parts of the world. Today, more than 200 million **Indigenous** people live all over the globe. Many still perform sacred ceremonies on the land. These members of the Wayuri tribe in Ecuador are waiting to play their drums for a welcoming ceremony.

These Bulgarian *kukeri* wear elaborate costumes and perform traditional rituals to ensure a good harvest for the village. Their wooden masks and metal bells are designed to ward off evil spirits.

Many long-ago customs have been lost over the centuries, but some are still practiced today – like celebrating the birth of a new baby, mourning the death of a community member, marking the change of the seasons, or healing someone who is injured or sick.

These three men are performing a *haka,* the Maori ceremonial dance used to welcome guests or honor important achievements. *Hakas* are performed by men, women, children, school groups, and sports teams.

Hindu Temples

Eventually, humans began building temples for their sacred rituals. Some of these early temple-builders followed a way of life called ***Sanatana Dharma*** {SAH-nuh-TAH-nuh DAR-muh}, commonly known as Hinduism.

Hindu temples come in all sorts of colors.

Some temples look brown or gray from the wood, bricks, or stones used to build them. This temple is part of the Ellora Cave complex in India. It has over 100 caves and many sacred spaces.

Some temples are painted bright white. This temple, found just outside Chicago, was built according to ancient, detailed instructions.

Other temples are painted in the colors of the rainbow. See the brightly-painted gods and goddesses in this close-up image of a temple in India?

Since the natural world is so important in Hinduism, temples are often built in beautiful settings – like on a mountain or near a lake – and the architecture is based on precise designs requiring accurate measurements.

Hindu temples also vary in shape. Some, like this one, have a single tower, which might make you think of a mountain or encourage your eyes to lift toward the sky. Others have lots of domes and towers. Can you count the domes and towers on the white temple?

The oldest Hindu temples, also called ***mandirs*** {man-deers}, are found in the land now known as India.

Hindus live all over the world. But, in India, about 80% of the population is Hindu. That's over 950 million people!

Before entering a temple, Hindus remove their shoes as a sign of respect.

Once inside, you almost always see a statue in the center of the room. Many Hindus believe in a Spiritual Oneness or Universal Essence found in all living things. That's hard to describe, so Hindus often use gods and goddesses to represent aspects of those ideas.

This Hindu **deity,** with the head of an elephant, is called Ganesh. Can you see his crown, fancy chair, colorful clothes, and jewelry? Those things show how special he is!

Many Hindus have home altars. Devout Hindus visit their altars every day to light a candle, say a prayer, offer flowers, burn incense, or sit for a few minutes of quiet meditation.

This Hindu man makes offerings at his home altar. The goddess statue is decorated with flower leis.

This young woman offers flowers and incense to Hindu **deities** at an outdoor temple in Bali, Indonesia.

Hindus might also visit temples where priests offer daily rituals. During these ***pujas*** {POO-juhs}, they chant hymns, recite ***mantras,*** and make offerings to **deities.**

Pujas usually end with a sacred ceremony called ***aarti*** {ah-ar-tee}. Candles are placed on a special plate and lit. Then, the plate is waved slowly in front of the **deities** as an offering.

These women offer fire/light and other gifts as part of an ***aarti*** ceremony.

Buddhist Temples

Buddhism also began in the country we now call India. Then, it spread throughout Asia. In fact, all the photos on these two pages were taken in countries where the majority of the population is Buddhist.

These ruins are from a temple in Cambodia called Angkor Thom {toom}, which means "Great City." Can you find the Buddha images carved into the stone?

This building, called the Shrine Hall, is part of a temple complex in Thailand. It is ornate and colorful both inside and out.

Like Hindu ***mandirs,*** many Buddhist temples are set in awe-inspiring locations. This temple in Bhutan was literally built on the side of a mountain.

Paro Taktsang {pah-roh tahkt-sahng} is also known as Tiger's Nest, but the actual translation of "taktsang" is "tigress lair." According to legend, a famous Buddhist teacher flew on the back of a tigress to the mountain cave that lies within the temple.

Dome-like towers, called ***stupas*** {stoo-puhs}, are another common feature of Buddhist temples. This Golden Pagoda in Burma (Myanmar) consists of one large **stupa** surrounded by several smaller ones.

Some ***stupas,*** like this one, hold sacred objects that have been preserved for a long time. These **relics,** which might include hair or teeth, are highly respected in some Buddhist traditions.

Buddhists follow the teachings and writings of the Buddha, meaning "Awakened One." He taught people to live with compassion, kindness, and mindfulness.

As a sign of respect, Buddhists, like Hindus, remove their shoes before entering a temple. Once inside, you'll almost always see a Buddha statue. You'll also sometimes see candles, incense, or even small water bowls on the altar.

Buddhists often pray for the peace and happiness of all living beings. Other customs, like bowing or making offerings of food, flowers and money, are ways to honor the Buddha's life and the wisdom of his ideas.

Listening to teachings from spiritual leaders, called ***gurus*** or ***lamas,*** is a common practice in the Buddhist tradition. Sitting meditation, either at home or in a temple, is another one.

Monks (men) and **nuns** (women) usually wear special clothes and live a simple life away from their families. They also spend most of their day studying, praying, and meditating. Many faith traditions have **monks** and **nuns,** but they are usually adults. In the Buddhist tradition, **monks** can begin their spiritual life even as young boys.

Unique practices from the Tibetan tradition, like prayer flags and sand ***mandalas,*** are now familiar to many people around the world.

In the Himalayan mountains, cloth prayer flags are made in these five colors. When they blow in the wind, the printed blessings are said to bring peace and good will to all.

Monks carefully apply colorful grains of sand to a ***mandala.*** The disassembling ceremony then offers the **mandala's** blessings to the world.

Christian Churches

In much of the world, the majority of people are part of the Christian traditions. Their sacred spaces are usually called churches. Big, fancy churches are also called cathedrals or basilicas. Sometimes, they have **relics,** like Buddhist **stupas.**

Cathedral of Saints Peter and Paul
Brno, Czech Republic

Dormition Cathedral
Moscow, Russia

Instead of being built near majestic places in nature, churches are often located in the center of towns or neighborhoods.

The symbol for Christianity is a cross. You almost always see crosses both on the outside and the inside of churches. Some churches are even built in the shape of a cross!

Many churches have domes on top – somewhat similar to those seen on temples. Do you see any domes on the churches pictured here?

Another typical feature seen on churches is a **steeple.** Some **steeples** have clocks, so everyone can see the time. And some **steeples** have bells that ring on Sunday mornings for services. Sometimes, the **steeple** has a **spire** on top, which points toward the heavens and makes the church even taller.

Can you find the **steeples** on all these churches?

Smaller, less ornate churches are sometimes called chapels. This wooden church built on the lava rock of Iceland is a good example.

Inside, you'll almost always see an altar at the front. Like temple altars, they often hold candles and flowers. But, you won't see gods, goddesses, or the Buddha. Instead, you might see images of Jesus and other people described in Christian Bibles.

This altar has flowers, candles, a cross, and a Bible.

Many churches have colorful windows made of small pieces of "stained" glass. They look quite vibrant when the sun shines through them. Can you find the stained glass window behind the altar?

Sometimes, Bible stories are illustrated in church paintings. This church has a stained-glass window with paintings on each side.

Most churches have long benches, called **pews,** where people sit and listen to the church leader – called a minister, priest, or pastor. Most churches also have books, called **hymnals,** that contain prayers and songs, so everyone can follow along and participate.

Can you find the...

crosses

altar

pews

hymnals

...in this church?

Jewish Synagogues

Jewish faith traditions existed long before Christianity. In fact, Jesus, the central figure in Christianity, was Jewish. In those times, the most important sacred space for Jews was the Temple of Jerusalem. The First Temple was destroyed in a war, so they built a Second Temple, which was also destroyed in a war.

This model of the Second Temple is based on historical descriptions. It's on display at the Israel Museum in Jerusalem.

These boys are praying at the **Western Wall,** one of the few remaining pieces of the Second Temple. Sometimes, people write prayers on slips of paper and place them in the cracks.

For Jews, praying and studying their sacred texts are important practices, and the Temple offered a place where they could come together, in community, for these rituals. Today, some Jews still call their sacred places temples, but they're also called **synagogues,** meaning "gathering spaces."

Like other sacred spaces, **synagogues** come in various shapes, sizes, and colors. Sometimes, they have domes or small towers.

Sometimes, they look like the places that surround them. And sometimes, they look more like regular buildings.

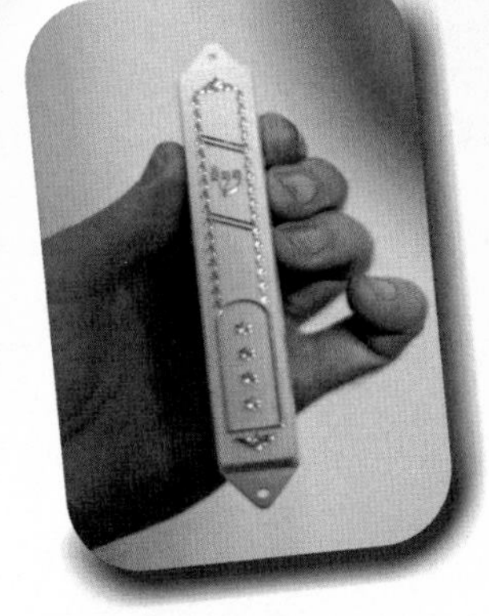

Mezuzahs, small pieces of special paper with notable prayers written on them, can be placed in decorative cases. They remind Jews of their relationship with God and are often put on the right-hand side of doors.

Synagogues and Jewish Centers have at least one ***mezuzah.*** Many Jews also put ***mezuzahs*** on the doors of their homes.

Once inside a **synagogue,** you'll see the *Aron Kodesh* {ah-ROHN KO-desh}, which means "holy cabinet." It's always found on the wall facing Jerusalem.

At special times during services, members of the congregation open and close the doors or curtains of the ***Aron Kodesh.*** Sometimes, they also face the ***Aron Kodesh*** to pray.

The ***Aron Kodesh*** holds the scrolls, which are hand-written copies of the first five books of the Bible, called the **Torah.**

A raised platform that sometimes looks a bit like a table, holds the scrolls when they are read. It's called a ***bimah*** {BIM-uh}. Can you find the ***Aron Kodesh*** and the ***bimah?***

The ***menorah,*** a candle-holder that holds seven to nine candles, is an important Jewish symbol. **Synagogues** always have at least one ***menorah.*** Nine-candle ***menorahs*** are also used during the Hanukkah holiday. Can you find two more ***menorahs*** on these pages?

Another important Jewish symbol, the **Star of David,** has six points and looks like two overlapping triangles. Can you see the triangles? Can you count the six points?

Many men and some women wear a small cap called a ***yarmulke*** {YAH-mah-kuh}, especially in **synagogues.** Can you see them on the boys praying at the **Western Wall?**

Jewish spiritual leaders are called **rabbis.** During services, they wear a special, fringed prayer shawl called a ***tallit*** *{tah-LEET}*. Some members of the congregation wear prayer shawls, too.

Islamic Mosques

In the Islamic traditions, sacred spaces are called **mosques.** People who follow Islam are called Muslims. They always face the city of Mecca when they pray. Many Muslims also visit their most important **mosque,** the Great Mosque in Mecca, at least once in their lifetimes.

In the center of the Great Mosque, stands the ***Kaaba*** {kah-bah}, a large cube covered with a black and gold cloth. In this image, thousands of people are walking around the **Kaaba.** See how small they look?

Mosques, called ***masjids*** {mas-jids} in Arabic, sometimes have domes, like temples and churches. Usually, they also have a **minaret** {min-uh-RET}, a small tower that looks a bit like a church **steeple.**

Yali Mosque in Izmir, Turkey

This is the Crystal Mosque found in Malaysia.
Can you count the domes and **minarets**?

Can you also see the crescent moons,
a symbol of Islam, on top of the **minarets**?

Minarets broadcast the Islamic call to prayer five times a day. Whenever devout Muslims hear the call, they stop what they're doing and pray – either at a **mosque** or anywhere else they happen to be.

The precise prayer times are determined by the sun's position in the sky. In this way, Islam is closely connected to nature, just like the Indigenous and Hindu traditions.

Before entering a **mosque,** Muslims prepare by washing their eyes, ears, nose, mouth, face, forearms, and feet with water. Nearly all women (and some men) cover their heads. They also remove their shoes, like the Hindu and Buddhist traditions.

This Muslim girl, already wearing her head covering, is washing before entering the **mosque.** In places where it's warm, these areas can be outdoors. In places where it gets cold, they are indoors.

Once inside a **mosque**, you'll see no elaborately-decorated gods or goddesses, no Buddhas, no illustrations of Bible stories, and no menorahs. Instead, **mosques** are adorned with colorful flowers, beautiful geometric designs, and fancy writing called **calligraphy.**

This decorative mosaic is made entirely of small tiles.

This is an Arabic phrase written in **calligraphy.** It's sometimes translated as "In the name of God, the Most Gracious, the Most Merciful."

Instead of altars, **mosques** have an alcove, called a ***mihrab*** {MEE-huh-rahb}. It shows the prayer direction. Many **mosques** also have a small staircase, called a ***minbar*** {MIN-bar}, for the spiritual leader. The ***imam*** {ee-mam} sits or stands at the top of the **minbar** for recitations and teachings.

Can you see the ***mihrab***? Can you see the ***minbar***? Can you see the tile mosaics?

The rest of the **mosque** is mostly open, carpeted space. Everyone stands in a line with shoulders touching. Then, everyone performs the different prayer postures at the same time. Women usually pray behind men.

These Muslim kids are praying on a decorated carpet or individual prayer mats. They have already removed their shoes. Also, both girls and some boys wear head-coverings.

Sikh Gurdwaras

The Sikh {sik} religion, like the Hindu and Buddhist traditions, also began in India. One of the most important words in the Sikh tradition is **guru** {GOO-roo} which means "wise teacher."

In fact, the word for Sikh temples is **gurdwara** {gur-DWAH-rah}, which means "gateway to the Guru."

This **gurdwara** in India, the Golden Temple, is the most revered and the most visited **gurdwara** in the world.

This **gurdwara** in England looks more like a regular building with domes added to the top.

Domes are clearly a popular feature of sacred spaces. Temples, churches, **mosques,** and Sikh **gurdwaras** all have them. Can you find all the domes on these **gurdwaras**?

Before entering a **gurdwara,** Sikhs remove their shoes, which is also what Hindus, Buddhists, and Muslims do before entering their sacred spaces. Sikh men and women also cover their heads as an additional sign of respect.

Some Sikhs keep their heads covered at all times, even when they're not in the **gurdwara,** by wearing turbans and/or headscarves.

Nearly all Sikh temples also have at least one flag pole on or near the **gurdwara.** It displays an orange or yellow flag with the Sikh symbol on it.

This symbol, called the ***Khanda*** {KAHN-duh}, represents the freedom and strength found in the One God. Can you find the flags flying near the Golden Temple?

There are many important **Gurus** in Sikhism. The Supreme Being, or Almighty God, is known as ***Waheguru*** {WAH-hay-GOO-roo}, which means "Wondrous Teacher."

Then there are ten human **Gurus** who built the Sikh community. They were wise leaders who lived according to the Sikh principles of unity, harmony, and equality.

The Sikh holy book, the ***Guru Granth Sahib*** {sah-heeb}, is also a **Guru!** It's kept on a raised platform that is sheltered by a canopy. Most of the time, it also sits on cushions and is covered with beautiful cloths.

Sikh spiritual leaders uncover the ***Guru Granth Sahib*** during worship services and read from it.

Musicians also lead in the singing of special hymns. Worshippers sit on the floor and join in. In some **gurdwaras,** men sit on one side and women sit on the other.

These kids are learning to play traditional Sikh instruments – the harmonium (pump organ) and the tabla (drums).

Sikhs, widely known for treating everyone equally, put their beliefs into practice with ***langars*** {LANG-ars}, which are kind of like free picnics.

Everyone eats on the floor, and no one is given a better seat or a better meal than anyone else. Hundreds, or even thousands, can be fed during a ***langar.*** And some Sikh **gurdwaras** have large spaces for hosting them.

See all the different scarves and turbans worn to cover their heads?

Conclusion

The world is full of sacred places. Many of them have been around for hundreds, or even thousands, of years.

Sometimes, people laugh, dance, eat, and celebrate in them. But even if everyone seems cheerful and excited to be there, sacred places always require a certain amount of awe and reverence. They're not places for running around or goofing off.

Instead, they're places for connecting with something deeper, or bigger, than ourselves. They're places where people can come together to pray, sing, meditate, chant, and learn. They're places deserving of deep respect. And each one is unique and special and sacred…just like you!

Thought Questions

Nature is very important for sacred spaces in Indigenous, Hindu, and Buddhist traditions. Is there a place in nature that's special to you?

In Hindu mandirs, Buddhist temples, Islamic mosques, and Sikh gurdwaras people remove their shoes in respect. Have you ever done that in a sacred space? Would you like to try it?

In Islamic mosques and Sikh gurdwaras people often cover their heads as a sign of respect. What do you think of that idea? If you covered your head, what would you wear?

Do you think the domes on the different sacred spaces are similar or different? What about towers, stupas, minarets, and steeples/spires?

Which is your favorite sacred space? Why?

Glossary

Aarti…offering light/fire to deities in the Sanatana Dharma/Hindu traditions (15)

Aron Kodesh…holy cabinet, found in Jewish synagogues on the wall facing Jerusalem (26)

Bimah…small table in Jewish synagogues that holds scrolls when read (26)

Calligraphy…artistic handwriting (usually in Arabic, in this case) often seen as a decorative element in mosques (30)

Deity…any supernatural being considered divine (7-8,14-15)

Elder...Indigenous man or woman, usually older in age, recognized for being wise; often known for being a healer and a keeper of ancestral legends (10)

Gurdwara…Sikh temple or place of worship (32, 33, 35)

Guru…spiritual teacher in Hindu, Buddhist, and Sikh traditions (18, 32-34)

Guru Granth Sahib…Sikh holy book; written in poetic verses that are often sung as hymns or prayers (34)

Hymnal…book containing songs that are sung by Christians during worship services (23)

Imam…faith leader in the Islamic tradition (31)

Indigenous…original inhabitants of a place (8, 10, 29)

Kaaba…large, sacred cube in the center of the Great Mosque of Mecca (28)

Khanda…symbol of the Sikh religion (33)

Lama...a learned teacher in the Tibetan Buddhist tradition (18)

Langar…free, vegetarian meal in the Sikh tradition that highlights the equality of all people (35)

Mandir…temple in the Sanatana Dharma/Hindu traditions (13, 17)

Mantra…word or sound that is chanted, often repeatedly (15)

Mandala...symbolic images, often circular, representing the cosmos (19)

Masjid...Arabic word for mosque (28)

Mezuzah...special paper with Jewish prayers; often placed in decorative cases and put on doorways (25)

Menorah...candle-holder in Jewish synagogues; also used during Hanukkah (27)

Mihrab…niche or alcove inside a mosque that indicates the prayer direction (toward Mecca) for Muslims; serves as the front of the prayer space; the minbar is always nearby. (31)

Minaret…tall slender tower built in or near a mosque; sounds the call to prayer five times a day (28-29)

Minbar…narrow staircase found inside a mosque and near the mihrab; raises the imam above the congregants (31)

Monk/Nun...someone who dedicates his/her life to a faith tradition; found in Hinduism, Buddhism, and Christianity (19)

Mosque…prayer space for Muslims who are part of the Islamic traditions (28-31)

Pew…long bench with a back where people sit; common in Christian churches and Jewish synagogues (23)

Puja…worship service or single ritual in the Sanatana Dharma/Hindu traditions (15)

Prayer Shawl…special fringed cloth, worn by rabbis and others, in Jewish synagogues (27)

Rabbi…faith leader in the Jewish tradition (27)

Relics...historical objects, usually from distinguished teachers or saints, that have been preserved; most common in Buddhist and Christian traditions (17, 20)

Santana Dharma…non-colonial term for Hinduism, a set of faith traditions that originated in what is now India (12)

Spire…pointed, tapering structure found atop Christian churches or steeples (21)

Star of David…six-pointed star; symbol of Judaism (27)

Steeple…tower on top of a building, especially Christian churches (21, 28)

Stupas...Buddhist structures, often pointed with a dome base, that may contain relics. Exterior stupas can be quite large. Interior stupas are smaller. (17, 20)

Synagogue…name of worship spaces in the Jewish traditions (25-27)

Tallit…Hebrew word for prayer shawl (27)

Torah…first five books of the Bible in the Jewish tradition (26)

Waheguru…the name of the Creator-God/Supreme Being in Sikhism (34)

Western Wall…portion of the Second Temple that remains as a Jewish place of prayer (24, 27)

Yarmulke…small cap worn by some Jews, especially in synagogues (27)

Additional Suggestions

Visiting Sacred Spaces

There's no substitute for actually visiting sacred spaces – either in the area where you live or while traveling. Finding faith communities is easy since most have web sites that include a calendar and photos. If you're feeling adventurous, show up for a service, ***puja,*** or holiday event. Some web sites even include visitor guidelines or answers to FAQs. If you're unsure about what to do or whether your presence is permissible, check in with a quick phone call or e-mail.

Visiting an unfamiliar sacred space helps your kids move outside their comfort zones while remaining respectful and compassionate. And, you'll be amazed by how much they can learn just by soaking up the sights, sounds, and smells of a new place. If a visit feels like too much, simply drive by and enjoy the building's exterior and grounds.

Researching Sacred Spaces on the Internet

Kids can also learn a fair amount on their smart phones/computers. Conduct internet searches for images of temples, churches, synagogues, **mosques,** and **gurdwaras**. Notice similarities and differences both within and across faith traditions. Or, simply explore web sites or Facebook pages curated by nearby houses of worship.

Many faith traditions also offer "101" web pages geared to kids. These sites often explain basic beliefs/practices and the significance of major holy days in age-appropriate language. Some sites are designed specifically for kids doing school-related research.

Reading About Sacred Spaces

Books about sacred spaces for each individual tradition are also available for all the world's major religions. Here are some titles to look for.

Indigenous Sites

Between Earth & Sky: Legends of Native American Sacred Places by Joseph Bruchac and Thomas Locker (HMH Books for Young Readers, 1999).

Many other non-fiction books focus on natural wonders of the world or specific sites. They tend to have a science/social science slant. Examples include:

Wonders of the World (DK: Eyewitness Series) by Tom Jackson (DK Children, 2014).

The Ganges: India's Sacred River (Rivers Around the World Series) by Molly Aloian (Crabtree Publishing, 2010).

Hindu/Sanatana Dharma Temples

Hindu Mandir (Places of Worship Series) by Angela Wood (Gareth Stevens Publishing, 2000).

Hindu Mandirs (Let's Find Out About Series) by Anita Ganeri (Heinemann-Raintree, 2005).

What You Will See Inside a Hindu Temple by Drs. Mehendra Jania and Vandana Jani with photographs by Neirah Bargava and Vijay Dave (SkyLight Paths, 2005).

Buddhist Temples

Buddhist Temple (Where We Worship Series) by Angela Wood (Watts Publishing Group, 2000).

Buddhist Temples (Let's Find Out About Series) by Anne Geldart (Heinemann-Raintree, 2005).

Christian Churches

Christian Church (Places of Worship Series) by Angela Wood (Gareth Stevens Publishing, 2000).

The Vatican and Other Christian Holy Places (Holy Places Series) by Victoria Parker (Heinemann Educational Books, 2002).

Jewish Synagogues

Jewish Synagogue (Places of Worship Series) by Angela Wood (Gareth Stevens Publishing, 2000).

Jewish Synagogue (Keystone Series) by Laurie Rosenberg (A & C Black, 2005).

Jewish Synagogues (Let's Find Out About Series) by Mandy Ross (Heinemann Educational Books, 2005).

Islamic Mosques

Muslim Mosque (Places of Worship Series) by Angela Wood (Gareth Stevens Publishing, 2000).

Visiting a Mosque (Start Up Religion Series) by Ruth Nason (The Creative Company, 2005).

What You Will See Inside a Mosque by Aisha Karen Khan and Aaron Pepis (SkyLight Paths, 2008).

Sikh Gurdwaras

Sikh Gurdwara (We Worship Here Series) by Kanwaljit Kaur-Singh (Franklin Watts, 2019).

Sikh Gurdwaras (Let's Find Out About Series) by Jane Bingham (Heinemann-Raintree, 2005).

Visiting a Gurdwara (Start Up Religion Series) by Kanwaljit Kaur-Singh and Ruth Nason (The Creative Company, 2005).

Image Credits

Introduction pp. 4-5

Two Boys Smiling by White77. Retrieved from https://pixabay.com/photos/boys-funny-faces-expressions-286179/.

Red-Haired Girl (Illustration) by Drawkman. Purchased from Dreamstime.

Group of Happy Kids by Erdenebayar. Retrieved from https://pixabay.com/photos/kids-smile-happy-children-young-977095/.

Boy in Wheelchair (Illustration) by Dannyphoto80. Purchased from Dreamstime.

African American Sisters by 5D Media. Retrieved from https://pixabay.com/photos/sisters-black-hair-hair-care-love-3484744/.

Introduction pp. 6-7

Stadium Crowd Giving Praise by Luis Quintero. Retrieved from https://www.pexels.com/photo/people-raising-hands-2019333/.

Bush Woman by Erich Wirz. Retrieved from https://pixabay.com/photos/woman-indigenous-smoking-smoke-470194/.

Muslim Girls Learning by WikiImages. Retrieved from https://pixabay.com/photos/girl-schoolgirl-learn-schulem-67694/.

Buddhist Girls Meditating by Honey Kochphon Onshawee. Retrieved from https://pixabay.com/photos/children-buddhists-tailor-seat-477878/.

Praying Hands and Sacred Text by Free-Photos. Retrieved from https://pixabay.com/photos/study-read-book-bible-koran-862994/.

Indigenous Sites pp. 8-9

Mount Mayon, Luzon, Philippines by Archie Binamira. Retrieved from https://www.pexels.com/photo/selective-focus-photographed-of-green-mountain-913215/.

Wave Rock, Hyden, Australia by RuRu_SG. Retrieved from https://pixabay.com/photos/west-australia-hyden-australia-wave-1966377/.

Painting of Ancient City of Petra, Jordan by Dawn Hudson. Purchased from Dreamstime.

Painting of Waterfall in Forest by Grandfailure. Purchased from Dreamstime.

Cave Painting, Baja California Sur, Mexico by rodro. Retrieved from https://pixabay.com/photos/cave-painting-prehistoric-rupestral-936619/.

Indigenous Sites pp. 10-11

Bonfire in Night Forest (Illustration) by GeoArt. Purchased from Shutterstock.

African Tribal Masks (Illustration) by HappyPictures. Purchased from Shutterstock.

Drummers, Wayuri Tribe. Personal photo.

Bulgarian Kukeri by GEORGID. Retrieved from https://pixabay.com/photos/bulgaria-costume-festival-games-3964838/.

Maorian Haka Dancers by Nydegger. Retrieved from https://pixabay.com/photos/maori-men-jump-hop-spear-fighter-113729/.

Hindu Temples pp. 12-13

Kailasa Hindu Temple, Aurangabad District, Maharashtra, India by sachinkawale. Retrieved from https://pixabay.com/photos/temple-kailas-temple-kailasatemple-3711082/.

BAPS Shri Swaminarayan Mandir, Bartlett, Illinois, USA by naturepost. Retrieved from https://pixabay.com/photos/baps-hindu-temple-religion-snow-1064932/.

Champakadhama Swamy Temple (close-up) by prasanna_devadas. Retrieved from https://pixabay.com/photos/hindu-panchalingeshwara-temple-2352121/.

Champakadhama Swamy Temple, Bangalore, Kanata, India by prasanna_devadas. Retrieved from https://pixabay.com/photos/hindu-panchalingeshwara-temple-2352119/.

Global Map of Hinduism by M Tracy Hunter. Retrieved (CC-BY-SA-3.0) from https://commons.wikimedia.org/wiki/File:Hinduism_percent_population_in_each_nation_World_Map_Hindu_data_by_Pew_Research.svg.

Hindu Temples pp. 14-15

Ganesh (Illustration) by GraphicsDNA. Purchased from Shutterstock.

Home Altar, Kolkata, India by Christina Kundu. Retrieved (CC-BY-SA-3.0) from https://commons.wikimedia.org/wiki/File:Puja_to_the_goddess.jpg.

Balinese Woman Praying by keulefm. Retrieved from https://pixabay.com/photos/indonesia-bali-woman-pray-temple-570661/.

Children Offering Aarti (Illustration). Purchased from Dreamstime.

Women Offering Aarti by Pramal. Retrieved (CC-BY-2.0) from https://commons.wikimedia.org/wiki/File:(1)_Aarti_Thali,_Prayer_Plate_India.jpg.

Buddhist Temples pp. 16-17

Angkor Thom, Cambodia by tomichinn. Retrieved from https://pixabay.com/photos/cambodia-baiao-angkor-thom-1338346/.

Phra That Choeng Chum, Thailand by naturepost. Retrieved from https://pixabay.com/photos/wat-phra-that-choeng-chum-the-temple-1193574/.

Paro Taktsang, Bhutan by Vikramjit Kakati. Retrieved fom https://pixabay.com/photos/the-tiger-s-nest-monastery-171377/.

Shwedagon Pagoda, Myanmar (Burma) by Aung Thu Soe. Retrieved from https://pixabay.com/photos/myanmar-yangon-pagoda-buddhism-4010558/.

Buddhist Temples pp. 18-19

Buddha Statue by susteh. Retrieved from https://pixabay.com/photos/buddha-buddhism-enlightenment-2919798/.

Paying Homage to Teachers by truthseeker08. Retrieved from https://pixabay.com/photos/theravada-buddhism-homage-faithfully-1807696/.

Girl Meditating by Honey Kochphon Onshawee. Retrieved from https://pixabay.com/photos/girl-buddhism-meditation-481259/.

Boy Monk by Sompoch Assawachotechuangkul. Retrieved from https://pixabay.com/photos/novice-buddhism-monks-religion-4479081/.

Prayer Flags by Wolfgang Eckert. Retrieved from https://pixabay.com/photos/flags-prayer-flags-sky-buddhism-3087921/.

Buddhist Monk Making Sand Mandala by Valeria Sangiovanni. Purchased from Dreamstime.

Christian Churches pp. 20-21

Cathedral of Saints Peter and Paul, Petrov, Brno, Czech Republic by romavor. Retrieved from https://pixabay.com/photos/brno-czech-republic-petrov-church-4335324/.
Dormition Cathedral, Vladimir, Russia by falco. Retrieved from https://pixabay.com/photos/church-dome-steeple-golden-russia-517514/.
Steeple (Illustration) by olegdogvan via fiverr.
Búðakirkja, Búðir, Iceland by Ronile. Retrieved from https://pixabay.com/photos/iceland-budakirkja-church-chapel-270411/.

Christian Churches pp. 22-23

Church Altar by geralt. Retrieved from https://pixabay.com/photos/church-gootehaus-altar-window-216842/.
Stained Glass Window (Illustration) by Fedor Labyntsev. Purchased from Dreamstime.
Stained Glass Window and Paintings by FelixMittermeier. Retrieved from https://pixabay.com/photos/church-prague-st-vitus-cathedral-3540869/.
Hymnal by Alexa Fotos. Retrieved from https://pixabay.com/photos/book-hymnal-church-pitched-1739068/.
Church Interior by Sylvea8. Retrieved from https://pixabay.com/photos/church-pews-spirituality-religion-2399965/.

Jewish Synagogues pp. 24-25

Model of Second Temple of Jerusalem by Berthold Werner. Retrieved from https://en.wikipedia.org/wiki/Holyland_Model_of_Jerusalem#/media/File:Jerusalem_Modell_BW_2.JPG.
Two Boys Praying at Western Wall by Aleks Megen. Retrieved from https://pixabay.com/photos/african-boy-prayer-western-wall-801512/.
Jubilee Synagogue, Prague, Czech Republic by Mikhail Markovskiy. Purchased from Shutterstock.
Spanish Synagogue, Prague, Czech Republic by Alberto Zamorano. Purchased from Shutterstock.
Person Holding Mezuzah by cottonbro. Retrieved from https://www.pexels.com/photo/person-holding-a-mezuzah-4034031/.

Jewish Synagogues pp. 26-27

Synagogue in Hobart, Australia by CutOffTies. Retrieved (CC-BY-SA-4.0) from https://commons.wikimedia.org/wiki/File:Hobart_Synagogue_Aron_Kodesh.jpg.
Torah Scroll, by falco. Retrieved from https://pixabay.com/photos/bible-torah-font-scroll-read-3524065/.
Grand Choral Synagogue, St. Petersburg, Russia by Iurii Spod. Retrieved from https://pixabay.com/photos/st-petersburg-russia-choral-synagogue-95128/.
Hanukkah Menorah by Blueenayim. Purchased from Dreamstime.
Star of David by Karen Arnold. Retrieved from https://pixabay.com/illustrations/star-of-david-star-jewish-symbol-938599/.
Prayer Shawl by DRosenbach. Retrieved from https://commons.wikimedia.org/wiki/File:Prayer_Shawl.JPG.

Islamic Mosques pp. 28-29

The Kaaba by Konevi. Retrieved from https://pixabay.com/photos/the-pilgrim-s-guide-religion-islam-4487889/.

Yali Mosque, Konak Square, Izmir, Turkey by 1508857. Retrieved from https://pixabay.com/photos/izmir-turkey-mansion-ege-square-990740/.

Crystal Mosque, Wan Man, Terrengganu, Malaysia by Dannysee. Retrieved from https://pixabay.com/.

Islamic mosque (Illustration) by taranajwahaura. Purchased from Dreamstime.

Islamic Mosques pp. 30-31

Muslim Girl Washing by Meoin Motlagh. Retrieved (CC-BY-4.0) from https://commons.wikimedia.org/wiki/File:Ramadan_Quran_Reading,_Bandar_Torkaman_(13950320163319583).jpg.

Bismillah (Illustration) by Warraich Sahib. Retrieved from https://commons.wikimedia.org/wiki/File:Bismillah_Calligraphy25.svg, Bismillah Calligraphy, Warraich Sahib.

Mosque Mosaic by Mike Van Acoleyen. Retrieved from https://pixabay.com/photos/mosaic-mosque-geometry-tile-rosas-583918/.

Mihrab and Minbar, al-Nasir Mohammad ibn Qalawun Mosque, Citadel, Cairo, Egypt by Khaled ElAdawy. Purchased from Shutterstock.

Muslim Kids Praying by Distinctiveimages. Purchased from Dreamstime.

Sikh Gurdwaras pp. 32-33

Golden Temple (Harmandir Sahib), Amritsar, Punjab by saiko3p. Purchased from Shutterstock.

Guru Nanak Darbar Gurdwara, Graveside, Kent, UK by Paul J Martin. Purchased from Shutterstock.

Gurdwara in New Delhi, India by A.Savin. Retrieved from https://commons.wikimedia.org/wiki/File:Gurudwara_Bangla_Sahib_in_New_Delhi_03-2016_img3.jpg.

Gurdwara, Khanda, and Two Sikhs Praying (Illustration) by pandora64. Purchased from Shutterstock.

Khanda (Illustration) by Fred the Oyster. Retrieved from https://commons.wikimedia.org/wiki/File:Khanda_emblem.svg.

Sikh Gurdwaras pp. 34-35

Guru Gobind Singh (Illustration) by olegdogvan via fiverr.

Gurdwara, Malaysian Region, Borneo by CEphoto, Uwe Aranas. Retrieved (CC-BY-SA-3.0) from https://commons.wikimedia.org/wiki/File:KotaKinabalu_Sabah_GurudwaraSahib-15.jpg.

Sikh Leader Reading from Guru Granth Sahib by Aakvik, Rune. Retrieved (CC-BY-SA-4.0) from https://commons.wikimedia.org/wiki/File:Sikh_med_hellig_skrift_i_Gurdwara_Sri_Guru_Nanak_Dev_Ji.jpeg.

Jaachak Kaur Teaching Kirtan During Summer Youth Camp at the Sikh Gurdwara, Raleigh, North Carolina, USA. Retrieved with permission from https://www.facebook.com/SikhGurudwaraNC/photos/a.1062329483809002/1671111586264119/?type=3&theater.

Langar in Gurdwara Bangla Sahib, New Delhi, India by Jean-Pierre Dalbéra. Retrieved (CC-BY-2.0) from https://commons.wikimedia.org/wiki/File:A_langar,_cuisine_communautaire_at_Gurdwara_Bangla_Sahib_New_Delhi_India_Inde.jpg.

Conclusion p. 36

Kids by Yannis H. Retrieved from https://unsplash.com/photos/uaPaEM7MiQQ.

Discussion Questions p. 37

Mountain landscape by Heidelbergerin. Retrieved from https://pixabay.com/photos/landscape-mountains-river-clouds-3632403/.

Shoes by AlinaDeng. Retrieved from https://pixabay.com/photos/temple-religion-worship-shoe-826227/.

Dome (Illustration). Retrieved from https://pixabary.com/vectors/cathedral-dome-building-religion-158153.

Acknowledgments

I am incredibly fortunate to have many friends, across many faith traditions, who educate, encourage, and tolerate me. Many, many thanks to those who helped with the faith-based aspects of this particular book: Yona FrenchHawk (Cherokee Wisdom Keeper); Joy Anna Hodges, Pandit Garlapati Sai Vara Prasad, and Lakshmi Anasuya Prasad Garlapati (Mount Soma and Sri Somesvara Temple); Dorje Lopön Dr. Hun Lye (Urban Dharma); Rochelle Reich (Congregation Beth Israel); Reda Ali and Farida Khan (Islamic Center of Asheville); Yasmin Soliman and Amro Elhelwa; and Rev. Ilene Kaur Tompkins-Gillispie.

Additional thanks to Jill Rose (Media Specialist, Charles C. Bell Elementary) and Jesse Figuera (Children's Librarian) for their wise input on overall content and design. Julieta Fumberg, graphic artist, also provided initial layout ideas.

About the Author

Vicki Michela Garlock attended a Lutheran grade school (Missouri Synod), a Lutheran church (ELCA) and a Catholic high school before receiving her Sc.B. in Psychology from Brown University. After earning her Ph.D. with dual specialties in neuroscience and cognitive development, she was a full-time Psychology Professor for over a decade.

In 2015, she founded Faith Seeker Kids (faithseekerkids.com) to provide churches, families, schools, and libraries with religious literacy resources for children of all ages. She's written almost 40 articles on various aspects of the interfaith world for The Interfaith Observer and makes regular contributions to Multicultural Kid Blogs.

From 2008 until the pandemic, she served as the Nurture Coordinator and Curriculum Specialist for Jubilee! Community Church. While there, she developed a multifaith curriculum for kids age preschool through 8th grade. Vicki was ordained as Jubilee's Minister of Education in 2018, and the Peace unit of her curriculum, also offered by Possibilities Publishing, was released in 2018-2019.

Vicki and her husband have two young-adult children and live in Asheville, NC.